미국 대입 필수 영단어

AMERICAN COLLEGE
VOCABULARY 101

HERMONHOUSE

"Give up making wishes. Instead, set goals."

소원 비는 일은 포기하라 대신,
목표를 세워라.

1	☐ abandon	버리다	forsake
2	☐ agile	민첩한	nimble
3	☐ archive	공적 기록	records
4	☐ berate	몹시 꾸짖다	criticize severely
5	☐ caliber	능력	capacity
6	☐ collusion	음모	plot
7	☐ contrite	회개하는	regretful
8	☐ deferential	공손한	respectful
9	☐ devoid	결여된	wanting
10	☐ distinctive	특이한	distinguishing
11	☐ embezzle	횡령하다	misappropriate
12	☐ eternal	영원한	timeless
13	☐ facsimile	복사	duplicate
14	☐ foil	좌절시키다	frustrate
15	☐ genteel	품위 있는	well-bred
16	☐ hallucination	환각	delusion
17	☐ hurtle	질주하다	dash
18	☐ imprudent	건방진	rude
19	☐ infectious	전염성의	contagious
20	☐ interrogation	심문	questioning
21	☐ keynote	기조	theme
22	☐ manipulate	교묘하게 조종하다	juggle
23	☐ misgiving	불안	uneasiness
24	☐ nettle	초조하게 만들다	upset
25	☐ oratory	웅변술	rhetoric
26	☐ pensive	생각에 잠긴	thoughtful
27	☐ predecessor	전임자	precursor
28	☐ reprehensible	비난할 만한	blameworthy
29	☐ rudimentary	기본의	fundamental
30	☐ skewed	왜곡된	crooked
31	☐ spatter	(물을) 튀기다	splash
32	☐ stringent	엄격한	exacting
33	☐ temperament	성격	personality
34	☐ temperance	금주	self-restraint
35	☐ velocity	속도	speed
36	☐ wrath	분노	ire

1	☐ abbreviate	줄이다	shorten
2	☐ aghast	경악한	shocked
3	☐ ardent	열정적인	fervid
4	☐ beseech	애원하다	implore
5	☐ callow	미숙한	immature
6	☐ colossal	거대한	immense
7	☐ convene	모이다	congregate
8	☐ deft	재빠른	agile
9	☐ devour	게걸스레 먹다	gobble
10	☐ distort	(형체나 모습을) 비틀다	deform
11	☐ embrace	포옹하다	hug
12	☐ etymology	어원학	word history
13	☐ faculty[1]	능력	talent
14	☐ foliage	나뭇잎	leaves
15	☐ gentry	상류 사회	aristocracy
16	☐ halt	멈추다	stop
17	☐ hub	중심지	center
18	☐ impudent	뻔뻔스러운	cheeky
19	☐ infernal	극도로 괴로운	hellish
20	☐ intersect	가로지르다	cross
21	☐ kidnap	유괴하다	abduct
22	☐ manual	손의	hand-operated
23	☐ mislead	속이다	misinform
24	☐ neutralize	효력을 없애다	counteract
25	☐ orchard	과수원	garden
26	☐ perceive	인식하다	recognize
27	☐ phony	가짜의	counterfeit
28	☐ quaint	기묘한	odd
29	☐ repress	억제하다	suppress
30	☐ shabby	초라한	run-down
31	☐ specific	구체적인	precise
32	☐ strive	노력하다	exert
33	☐ tarnish	녹슬게 하다	blemish
34	☐ trim	다듬다	curtail
35	☐ vend	팔다	peddle
36	☐ winnow	골라내다	sieve

1	☐ abdicate	(권리 등을) 버리다	abandon
2	☐ agitate	자극하다	instigate
3	☐ arduous	힘든	difficult
4	☐ besiege	에워싸다	surround
5	☐ callous	무감각한	insensitive
6	☐ comatose	혼수 상태의	unconscious
7	☐ dawdle	꾸물거리다	delay
8	☐ defiance	반항	resistance
9	☐ dexterous	(손이나 몸놀림이) 재빠른	proficient
10	☐ distracted	산만해진	disturbed
11	☐ embroidery	자수	fancy stitching
12	☐ eulogy	찬미	tribute
13	☐ faculty	강사진	teaching staff
14	☐ foolhardy	무모한	reckless
15	☐ genuine	진짜의	authentic
16	☐ hamlet	작은 마을	small village
17	☐ hustle	난폭하게 밀치다	jostle
18	☐ impugn	비난하다	assail
19	☐ infiltrate	침투 시키다	penetrate
20	☐ interval	(장소나 시간의) 간격	gap
21	☐ limb	팔과 다리	extremity
22	☐ manuscript	필사본	document
23	☐ mitigate	완화하다	alleviate
24	☐ nuisance	성가신 사람	annoyance
25	☐ ordeal	시련	trouble
26	☐ perennial	다년생의	enduring
27	☐ preface	책의 서문	foreword
28	☐ qualm	양심의 가책	misgiving
29	☐ reprimand	공개적으로 꾸짖다	blame
30	☐ rumple	구기다	crumple
31	☐ sham	거짓	pretense
32	☐ stroll	이리저리 거닐기	walk
33	☐ tart	맛이 시큼한	sour
34	☐ trip	발에 걸려 넘어지다	fall
35	☐ venerate	존경하다	revere
36	☐ wriggle	꿈틀거리며 움직이다	crawl

1	☐ abash	무안하게 하다	embarrass
2	☐ affront	모욕	insult
3	☐ arid	건조한	parched
4	☐ bestow	주다	give
5	☐ camouflage	가장하다	conceal
6	☐ comprehensive	포괄적인	inclusive
7	☐ conventional	관습적인	customary
8	☐ deficient	모자라는	insufficient
9	☐ despise	경멸하다	scorn
10	☐ distress	고통	suffering
11	☐ eminent	저명한	prominent
12	☐ euphemism	완곡 어법	circumlocution
13	☐ fainthearted	소심한	cowardly
14	☐ forage	마구 뒤지며 찾다	scavenge
15	☐ getaway	도주	escape
16	☐ hamper[1]	방해하다	hinder
17	☐ hybrid	잡종	mongrel
18	☐ impunity	처벌 받지 않음	exemption
19	☐ inflame	화나게 하다	excite
20	☐ intervene	사이에 끼어들다	arbitrate
21	☐ limerick	리머릭	verse
22	☐ mar	망치다	injure
23	☐ mnemonic	기억을 돕게 만드는 말이나 방법	cue
24	☐ nimble	민첩한	adroit
25	☐ perfunctory	아무렇게나 하는	desultory
26	☐ prejudiced	편견을 가진	biased
27	☐ quandary	당황	difficulty
28	☐ reproach	비난하다	censure
29	☐ rustic	시골 풍의	rural
30	☐ shard	(유리 등의) 조각	fragment
31	☐ specter	유령	ghost
32	☐ superfluous	불필요한	unnecessary
33	☐ taut	팽팽한	tight
34	☐ trite	흔한	clichéd
35	☐ venomous	독이 있는	malicious
36	☐ writhe	괴로워서 몸부림치다	twist

1	☐ abhor	몹시 싫어하다	detest
2	☐ akin	유사한	similar
3	☐ armada	함대	fleet
4	☐ bewildered	당황한	confounded
5	☐ candid	솔직한	frank
6	☐ converge	한 점으로 모이다	concentrate
7	☐ deflect	방향을 바꾸다	bounce off
8	☐ didactic	교훈적인	instructive
9	☐ diverge	갈라지다	branch off
10	☐ emit	발산하다	discharge
11	☐ euphoria	행복감	elation
12	☐ force	힘	power
13	☐ germane	적절한	relevant
14	☐ hamper[2]	바구니	container
15	☐ hyperbole	과장법	exaggeration
16	☐ imprint	각인	signature
17	☐ inflammable	가연성의	flammable
18	☐ intimate[1]	친한	close
19	☐ kindle	불이 붙다	ignite
20	☐ limp	흐느적거리는	flabby
21	☐ malignant	악성의	diseased
22	☐ maraud	약탈하다	plunder
23	☐ nocturnal	밤의	nightly
24	☐ ornamental	장식적인	decorative
25	☐ peril	큰 위험	danger
26	☐ preliminary	준비의	initial
27	☐ quarry[1]	채석장	pit
28	☐ reprove	타이르다	admonish
29	☐ rustle	살랑살랑 소리 내다	swish
30	☐ sheath	칼집	cover
31	☐ stalwart	충실한	sturdy
32	☐ stronghold	요새	bulwark
33	☐ tedious	지루한	boring
34	☐ trivial	하찮은	unimportant
35	☐ veracity	진실	truthfulness
36	☐ wry	비꼬는	sarcastic

1	☐ abominable	지긋지긋한	hateful
2	☐ alacrity	활발	liveliness
3	☐ aroma	향기	fragrance
4	☐ biased	선입견이 있는	prejudiced
5	☐ cantankerous	심술궂은	contentious
6	☐ commencement	시작	start
7	☐ convert	바꾸다	switch
8	☐ defunct	사용되지 않는	extinct
9	☐ degenerate	퇴보하다	worsen
10	☐ diction	어법	choice of words
11	☐ empathy	공감	understanding
12	☐ evade	피하다	avoid
13	☐ far-fetched	믿기지 않는	unlikely
14	☐ hangar	격납고	garage
15	☐ hypnotize	최면을 걸다	spellbind
16	☐ inadvertent	고의가 아닌	unintentional
17	☐ infringe	어기다	violate
18	☐ intimate^2	암시하다	imply
19	☐ kindred	관련된	related
20	☐ lineage	혈통	pedigree
21	☐ marginal	미미한	slight
22	☐ moderate	절제 있는	temperate
23	☐ nomad	유목민	wanderer
24	☐ ornate	화려하게 장식한	fancy
25	☐ paradigm	전형적인 예	example
26	☐ prelude	서곡	introduction
27	☐ quarry^2	사냥감	game
28	☐ repudiate	거절하다	disclaim
29	☐ ruthless	무자비한	cruel
30	☐ shed^1	오두막	hovel
31	☐ speculate	사색하다	conjecture
32	☐ stunning	굉장히 멋진	marvelous
33	☐ teem	충만하다	swarm
34	☐ trot	빠른 걸음으로 가다	jog
35	☐ verbalize	말로 표현하다	communicate
36	☐ xenophobia	이방인 공포증	fear of strangers

1	☐ aboveboard	정정당당한	honest
2	☐ affinity	친밀감	liking
3	☐ arouse	일깨우다	awaken
4	☐ bigoted	고집 센	opinionated
5	☐ candor	솔직함	honesty
6	☐ commiserate	위로하다	condole
7	☐ convincing	설득력 있는	assuring
8	☐ deity	신	god
9	☐ diffident	수줍은	timid
10	☐ diversion	기분 전환	recreation
11	☐ emphatic	어조가 강한	forceful
12	☐ evanescent	덧없는	transitory
13	☐ fallacy	그릇된 생각	misconception
14	☐ foreboding	예감	omen
15	☐ ghetto	빈민가	slum
16	☐ haphazard	아무렇게나	random
17	☐ hypocrisy	위선	insincerity
18	☐ inalienable	떨어뜨릴 수 없는	inviolable
19	☐ infirmity	병약	frailty
20	☐ intimidate	협박하다	browbeat
21	☐ lenient	관대한	tolerant
22	☐ mandatory	법에 정해진	obligatory
23	☐ modest	겸손한	humble
24	☐ nonchalant	무관심한	casual
25	☐ ostentatious	자랑 삼아 드러내는	showy
26	☐ penury	극빈	destitution
27	☐ premiere	초연	opening
28	☐ queasy	멀미하는 것 같은	nauseous
29	☐ repulse	격퇴하다	repel
30	☐ safeguard	안전 장치	protection
31	☐ shed²	흘리다	drop
32	☐ shiver	(몸을) 떨다	shake
33	☐ studious	열심인	diligent
34	☐ temperate	절제하는	moderate
35	☐ truant	무단결석자	absentee
36	☐ verbose	말이 많은	garrulous

1	☐ abridge	요약하다	abbreviate
2	☐ allocate	할당하다	assign
3	☐ arable	경작이 가능한	farmable
4	☐ bilk	속이다	deceive
5	☐ capitulate	항복하다	surrender
6	☐ commotion	동요	agitation
7	☐ convoluted	꼬인	coiled
8	☐ delegate	대표	deputy
9	☐ diffuse	퍼지다	disseminate
10	☐ divulge	폭로하다	reveal
11	☐ empirical	경험적인	experiential
12	☐ evict	내쫓다	expel
13	☐ fallow	묵히고 있는	uncultivated
14	☐ foresee	예견하다	anticipate
15	☐ homage	경의	reverence
16	☐ idealistic	이상주의적인	illusory
17	☐ inane	어리석은	silly
18	☐ ingenious	독창적인	clever
19	☐ kinetic	운동의	moving
20	☐ linger	망설이다	dawdle
21	☐ masquerade	가면 무도회	disguise
22	☐ mortify	굴욕감을 주다	humiliate
23	☐ noncommittal	애매한	evasive
24	☐ ostracize	추방하다	banish
25	☐ plebeian	평민의	base
26	☐ premonition	전조	foreboding
27	☐ quell	진압하다	vanquish
28	☐ reputable	이름 높은	respectable
29	☐ sage	현명한 사람	pundit
30	☐ sheen	광택	shine
31	☐ splice	밧줄을 꼬아 잇다	conjoin
32	☐ stupendous	놀라운	wonderful
33	☐ tempest	폭풍	storm
34	☐ trudge	터벅터벅 걷다	plod
35	☐ verdict	평결	decision
36	☐ zany	우스꽝스러운	funny

1	☐ absolve	용서하다	pardon
2	☐ affiliated	연계된	associated
3	☐ articulate	똑똑히 발음하다	enunciate
4	☐ bizarre	이상한	strange
5	☐ capricious	변덕스러운	unpredictable
6	☐ compelling	설득력 있는	fascinating
7	☐ criterion	판단 기준	standard
8	☐ deleterious	해로운	damaging
9	☐ digress	산만하게 굴다	stray
10	☐ docile	순종적인	pliant
11	☐ emulate	열심히 흉내 내다	mimic
12	☐ evince	명시하다	show
13	☐ falter	비틀거리다	stumble
14	☐ forestall	미리 손쓰다	prevent
15	☐ giggle	낄낄 웃다	snicker
16	☐ idiosyncratic	특유한	eccentric
17	☐ inanimate	무생물의	lifeless
18	☐ ingenuity	영리함	inventiveness
19	☐ intoxicating	취하게 하는	exhilarating
20	☐ knack	기술	ability
21	☐ massive	매우 큰	bulky
22	☐ molt	털을 갈다	exfoliate
23	☐ nondescript	정체를 알 수 없는	undistinguished
24	☐ outburst	감정의 폭발	burst
25	☐ perish	멸망하다	die
26	☐ preoccupied	몰두한	absorbed
27	☐ quench	갈증을 해소하다	extinguish
28	☐ retaliate	받은 대로 되갚아 주다	revenge
29	☐ salute	인사	greeting
30	☐ sheepish	수줍어하는	ashamed
31	☐ splinter	쪼개진 조각	piece
32	☐ sturdy	두껍고 억세 보이는	strong
33	☐ thrust	(거칠게) 밀다	push hard
34	☐ tumble	헛디뎌 넘어지다	descend
35	☐ verify	증명하다	validate
36	☐ zeal	열성	passion

1	☐ abstain	자제하다	forgo
2	☐ allay	고통을 줄여주다	mitigate
3	☐ asperity	혹독함	severity
4	☐ blackmail	공갈하다	threaten
5	☐ carnivorous	육식의	meat-eating
6	☐ compensate	보상하다	recompense
7	☐ coordinate	배열하다	harmonize
8	☐ deliberate	고의적인	intentional
9	☐ dilapidated	황폐한	ramshackle
10	☐ doctrine	종교 교리	principle
11	☐ enchant	매혹하다	captivate
12	☐ evoke	일깨우다	arouse
13	☐ famine	기근	starvation
14	☐ forewarn	미리 경고하다	caution
15	☐ gimmick	비밀 장치	scheme
16	☐ ignite	불을 붙이다	kindle
17	☐ inattentive	부주의한	negligent
18	☐ ingenuous	솔직 담백한	artless
19	☐ intrusion	침해	invasion
20	☐ knave	악당	rascal
21	☐ liquidate	(빚 등을) 청산하다	pay
22	☐ momentary	잠깐 동안의	brief
23	☐ nominal	명목상의	titular
24	☐ outdated	구식의	obsolete
25	☐ perjury	위증	lie
26	☐ plastic	형태를 만들기가 쉬운	malleable
27	☐ query	질문	question
28	☐ requisite	필요한	necessary
29	☐ salvation	구조	deliverance
30	☐ shimmer	부드럽게 빛나다	gleam
31	☐ spontaneous	자발적인	impulsive
32	☐ subdue	정복하다	quell
33	☐ tenable	공격에 견딜 수 있는	secured
34	☐ tumult	소동	uproar
35	☐ vernacular	자국어의	dialect
36	☐ zealot	열광자	partisan

1	☐ abstract	개요	summary
2	☐ allege	강력히 주장하다	claim
3	☐ aspire	간절히 원하다	yearn
4	☐ blanch	하얗게 만들다	whiten
5	☐ carnage	대학살	massacre
6	☐ competent	능력 있는	capable
7	☐ copious	풍부한	abundant
8	☐ delineate	윤곽을 그리다	describe
9	☐ dilemma	딜레마	perplexity
10	☐ dodge	재빨리 피하다	evade
11	☐ encompass	둘러싸다	include
12	☐ evolve	서서히 발전시키다	develop
13	☐ fanatic	광신자	maniac
14	☐ feud	(오랜 동안의) 불화	conflict
15	☐ gird	허리에 차다	encircle
16	☐ ignoble	저열한	mean
17	☐ inaugurate	정식으로 시작하다	initiate
18	☐ ingrained	뿌리 깊이 박힌	entrenched
19	☐ intrepid	겁 없는	fearless
20	☐ knead	반죽하다	blend
21	☐ listless	생기 없는	languid
22	☐ momentous	매우 중요한	important
23	☐ nonplussed	어찌 할 바를 모르는	confused
24	☐ outlandish	이국적인	exotic
25	☐ permanent	영원한	constant
26	☐ prescription	처방전	instruction
27	☐ quest	탐험	mission
28	☐ resent	분개하다	begrudge
29	☐ sanitary	위생의	hygienic
30	☐ soundness	건전성	healthiness
31	☐ sporadic	때때로 일어나는	intermittent
32	☐ submerge	물에 잠그다	dive
33	☐ tenacious	고집하는	pertinacious
34	☐ turbulence	거칠게 몰아침	tumult
35	☐ verse	운문	poetry
36	☐ zenith	정점	peak

1	☐ abstruse	난해한	unfathomable
2	☐ alleviate	고통을 줄여주다	abate
3	☐ artifice	책략	wile
4	☐ bland	맛이 밍밍한	flavorless
5	☐ cascade	작은 폭포	waterfall
6	☐ complacent	현실에 안주하는	contented
7	☐ cordial	마음에서 우러난	heartfelt
8	☐ deliverance	구출	salvation
9	☐ dilatory	지체하는	belated
10	☐ dogged	완고한	persistent
11	☐ encounter	우연히 만나다	come across
12	☐ exacerbate	더욱 심하게 하다	aggravate
13	☐ fanciful	변덕스러운	fickle
14	☐ forgo	없이 지내다	abstain
15	☐ genuflect	절하다	bow
16	☐ hazardous	위험한	risky
17	☐ ignominy	치욕	disgrace
18	☐ inhabit	살다	occupy
19	☐ intricate	복잡한	complicated
20	☐ knoll	둔덕	mound
21	☐ literacy	읽고 쓸 줄 아는 능력	knowledge
22	☐ maritime	바다의	nautical
23	☐ momentum	움직이게 하는 힘	impetus
24	☐ nostalgia	향수	reminiscence
25	☐ outlook	조망	viewpoint
26	☐ perfidy	배신	treachery
27	☐ quota	몫	allocation
28	☐ reserved	속 마음을 드러내지 않는	aloof
29	☐ sanctimonious	독실한 체하는	insincere
30	☐ shove	떠밀다	push
31	☐ sprint	전속력으로 달리다	run
32	☐ submissive	복종하는	obedient
33	☐ tenant	세입자	occupant
34	☐ turmoil	소란	confusion
35	☐ vertex	최고점	apex
36	☐ zephyr	서풍	breeze

1	☐ absurd	터무니없는	ridiculous
2	☐ alliance	동맹	union
3	☐ assertive	자기 주장이 강한	self-assured
4	☐ blasé	심드렁한	bored
5	☐ celerity	민첩함	swiftness
6	☐ compatible	잘 어울릴 수 있는	harmonious
7	☐ devout	독실한	pious
8	☐ dilute	묽게 하다	thin
9	☐ dogmatic	독단적인	dictatorial
10	☐ encumber	방해하다	hamper
11	☐ exalt	위로 떠받들다	glorify
12	☐ fetch	가지고 오다	return with
13	☐ formidable	무서운	horrible
14	☐ glance	힐끗 보다	glimpse
15	☐ hapless	불운한	unlucky
16	☐ ignorance	무지	unawareness
17	☐ incendiary	방화의	inflammatory
18	☐ inhumane	비인간적인	brutal
19	☐ intuition	직감	instinct
20	☐ knotty	복잡한	complex
21	☐ literal	글자대로의	exact
22	☐ milieu	(사회적) 환경	surroundings
23	☐ notable	유명한	renowned
24	☐ outpost	전초지	frontier
25	☐ perpetrate	나쁜 짓을 범하다	commit
26	☐ prestigious	고급의	honored
27	☐ quirk	기벽	idiosyncrasy
28	☐ resigned	단념한	reconciled
29	☐ sanction	승인하다	authorize
30	☐ showy	화려한	ostentatious
31	☐ spur	박차를 가하다	goad
32	☐ subordinate	부하	assistant
33	☐ tenet	집단이 신봉하는 주의	doctrine
34	☐ turncoat	변절자	betrayer
35	☐ veer	방향을 홱 틀다	swerve
36	☐ zest	열성	ardor

1	☐ abundant	풍부한	plentiful
2	☐ allusion	암시	implication
3	☐ assess	가치를 평가하다	appraise
4	☐ blast	거센 폭발	gale
5	☐ catastrophe	대재앙	calamity
6	☐ compliant	유순한	docile
7	☐ corpse	시체	dead body
8	☐ deluge	대홍수	downpour
9	☐ diminutive	아주 작은	tiny
10	☐ doldrums	답답함	depression
11	☐ encyclopedia	백과사전	reference book
12	☐ exasperated	분노한	irritated
13	☐ fastidious	까다로운	finicky
14	☐ fortify	강화시키다	strengthen
15	☐ glare	노려보다	stare
16	☐ hatchet	손도끼	ax
17	☐ illegitimate	위법의	unlawful
18	☐ inception	발단	beginning
19	☐ iniquity	부정	wickedness
20	☐ inundate	범람시키다	flood
21	☐ label	라벨을 붙이다	tag
22	☐ literary	문학의	fictional
23	☐ maternal	어머니의	motherly
24	☐ mongrel	잡종	hybrid
25	☐ notion	개념	belief
26	☐ outrage	분노	rage
27	☐ perpetual	영원한	everlasting
28	☐ preposterous	말도 안 되는	absurd
29	☐ resilient	원상태로 돌아가는	elastic
30	☐ sanctuary	보호구역	reserve
31	☐ shred	갈기갈기 찢다	tear
32	☐ spurious	가짜의	fake
33	☐ subsequent	다음의	following
34	☐ table	미루다	postpone
35	☐ tentative	시험적인	provisional
36	☐ vestige	자취	trace

1	☐ afflict	괴롭히다	bother
2	☐ aloof	냉담한	indifferent
3	☐ assiduous	지치지 않는	industrious
4	☐ blatant	명백한	obvious
5	☐ cater	제공하다	provide
6	☐ compliment	찬사	accolade
7	☐ corpulent	뚱뚱한	obese
8	☐ delusion	속임	deception
9	☐ dingy	우중충한	grimy
10	☐ doleful	슬픈	rueful
11	☐ endeavor	노력하다	attempt
12	☐ excess	초과	overabundance
13	☐ fathom	이해하다	understand
14	☐ fortitude	용기	determination
15	☐ glean	(정보 등을) 조금씩 모으다	collect
16	☐ haughty	오만한	arrogant
17	☐ iconoclast	우상 파괴자	nonconformist
18	☐ incessant	끊임없는	ceaseless
19	☐ initiate	시작하다	commence
20	☐ insofar	~하는 한에 있어서는	to such an extent
21	☐ laborious	힘든	onerous
22	☐ majesty	장엄함	grandeur
23	☐ maternity	모성	motherhood
24	☐ monitor	지켜보다	check
25	☐ novel	새로운	new
26	☐ overbearing	거만한	domineering
27	☐ perplex	난처하게 하다	bewilder
28	☐ presumptuous	주제넘은	audacious
29	☐ quintessence	핵심	essence
30	☐ recluse	은둔자	hermit
31	☐ seasoned	경험 많은	experienced
32	☐ shrewd	기민한	sharp
33	☐ spurn	쫓아내다	reject
34	☐ subservient	비굴한	submissive
35	☐ tenuous	희박한	feeble
36	☐ vessel	배	ship

1	☐ abyss	끝없는 심연	gulf
2	☐ alter	바꾸다	convert
3	☐ assuage	누그러뜨리다	relieve
4	☐ bleak	암담한	murky
5	☐ chamber	방	room
6	☐ complimentary	무료의	free
7	☐ correspondence	일치	similarity
8	☐ demise	죽음	death
9	☐ diplomatic	외교적 수완이 있는	tactful
10	☐ domicile	거주지	abode
11	☐ endorse	승인하다	affirm
12	☐ excruciating	고문받는 것 같은	torturous
13	☐ fatigue	피로	tiredness
14	☐ fortnight	2주간	fourteen nights
15	☐ grope	더듬다	fumble
16	☐ haul	세게 잡아 당기다	drag
17	☐ illicit	불법의	illegal
18	☐ incense	몹시 화나게 하다	enrage
19	☐ initiative	솔선	leadership
20	☐ irritable	짜증을 잘 내는	cranky
21	☐ lackluster	광택을 잃은	dull
22	☐ lithe	나긋나긋한	supple
23	☐ mayhem	신체 상해	violence
24	☐ mollify	달래다	pacify
25	☐ novice	초보자	beginner
26	☐ overdue	기한이 넘은	late
27	☐ persecution	박해	harassment
28	☐ pretentious	가식적인	affected
29	☐ quixotic	돈키호테 같은	visionary
30	☐ resonant	소리가 울리는	echoing
31	☐ sarcastic	빈정대는	satirical
32	☐ snub	무시하다	ignore
33	☐ subside	아래로 가라앉다	collapse
34	☐ tepid	미지근한	lukewarm
35	☐ twine	꼬다	coil
36	☐ veto	거부권	rejection

1	☐ accelerate	가속하다	speed up
2	☐ altercation	언쟁	argument
3	☐ assorted	여러 가지의	various
4	☐ boycott	구매나 사용을 거부하다	ban
5	☐ champion	옹호하다	advocate
6	☐ concede	인정하다	admit
7	☐ corroborate	확인하다	confirm
8	☐ demeanor	처신	behavior
9	☐ dire	무서운	dreadful
10	☐ drawback	결점	disadvantage
11	☐ endowment	기부금	gift
12	☐ excursion	야유회	expedition
13	☐ fatuous	얼빠진	foolish
14	☐ foster	양육하다	nurture
15	☐ galactic	거대한	huge
16	☐ haven	피난처	shelter
17	☐ illiterate	문맹의	uneducated
18	☐ incision	절개	cut
19	☐ inkling	눈치챔	hint
20	☐ invaluable	값을 헤아릴 수 없는	priceless
21	☐ lad	젊은이	boy
22	☐ litigation	소송	lawsuit
23	☐ matriculate	대학에 입학하다	enroll
24	☐ monologue	독백	monodrama
25	☐ noxious	유해한	harmful
26	☐ overhaul	정밀 검사하다	mend
27	☐ perseverance	인내	persistence
28	☐ piquant	톡 쏘는 듯한	pungent
29	☐ relentless	수그러들지 않는	merciless
30	☐ resort	의지	alternative
31	☐ shrine	성소	altar
32	☐ squander	돈을 펑펑 쓰다	waste
33	☐ surge	급증	deluge
34	☐ terminate	완전히 끝내다	end
35	☐ truncate	길이를 줄이다	cut short
36	☐ viable	생존 가능한	feasible

1	☐ accolade	칭찬	award
2	☐ altruistic	이타적인	philanthropic
3	☐ astounding	몹시 놀라게 하는	astonishing
4	☐ blight	망치다	mar
5	☐ chaotic	혼돈된	disorganized
6	☐ composed	평온한	tranquil
7	☐ corrosion	부식	disintegration
8	☐ debacle	대실패	catastrophe
9	☐ disapproving	불만스런	complaining
10	☐ dismay	크게 실망시키다	disappoint
11	☐ enervate	기력을 빼앗다	weaken
12	☐ execute	(직무나 계획을) 실행하다	carry out
13	☐ fauna	동물군	animals
14	☐ founder	가라앉다	sink
15	☐ glut	과잉	surfeit
16	☐ havoc	대규모의 황폐	ruin
17	☐ illuminate	비추다	brighten
18	☐ incisive	예리한	intelligent
19	☐ innate	타고난	inborn
20	☐ invective	심한 독설이나 비난	verbal abuse
21	☐ laden	(짐을) 잔뜩 실은	loaded
22	☐ litter	어질러 놓다	strew
23	☐ monopoly	독점	exclusive ownership
24	☐ nuance	뉘앙스	subtlety
25	☐ overhear	우연히 듣게 되다	monitor
26	☐ prevalent	일반적으로 행해지는	common
27	☐ proportion	부분	ratio
28	☐ rabble	오합지졸	mob
29	☐ redeem	만회하다	compensate
30	☐ satire	풍자	sarcasm
31	☐ shun	피하다	eschew
32	☐ stipulate	규정하다	designate
33	☐ substantiate	증거를 들어 입증하다	prove
34	☐ terminology	용어	terms
35	☐ tyro	초보자	amateur
36	☐ vibrant	활기 넘치는	lively

1	☐ acclaim	갈채	applause
2	☐ amass	쌓다	gather
3	☐ astute	예리한	perceptive
4	☐ blinding	눈을 멀게 할 만큼 강한 빛의	dazzling
5	☐ compulsory	필수적인	required
6	☐ cosmopolitan	전 세계적인	ecumenical
7	☐ demur	이의를 제기하다	protest
8	☐ disarming	상대방을 무장 해제시키는	charming
9	☐ drab	칙칙한	colorless
10	☐ epicure	미식가	gourmet
11	☐ exemplary	모범적인	outstanding
12	☐ feint	상대방을 속이는 동작	mock attack
13	☐ fraction	파편	part
14	☐ glum	침울한	sullen
15	☐ headlong	무모한	impetuous
16	☐ impale	찌르다	pierce
17	☐ incite	자극하다	provoke
18	☐ innocuous	해가 없는	harmless
19	☐ inventory	재고 목록	stock
20	☐ lag	뒤에 처지다	retard
21	☐ longevity	장수	durability
22	☐ meager	빈약한	scanty
23	☐ monotonous	단조로운	tedious
24	☐ nudge	(팔꿈치로 쿡) 찌르다	poke
25	☐ overlook	보고도 못 본 체하다	condone
26	☐ perspective	견해	outlook
27	☐ proprietor	소유주	owner
28	☐ radiant	환한	beaming
29	☐ respiration	호흡	breathing
30	☐ saturate	푹 적시다	impregnate
31	☐ sift	체로 치다	sort
32	☐ stagnant	흐르지 않는	stationary
33	☐ surrogate	대리인	proxy
34	☐ terrestrial	육지의	earthly
35	☐ ubiquitous	동시에 도처에 있는	omnipresent
36	☐ vicinity	근처	proximity

1	☐ accommodating	호의적인	obliging
2	☐ ambiguous	모호한	vague
3	☐ asylum	정신병원	haven
4	☐ bliss	완전한 행복	joy
5	☐ catholic	폭 넓은	broad-minded
6	☐ charlatan	사기꾼	quack
7	☐ conceal	감추다	hide
8	☐ demure	얌전 피우는	modest
9	☐ disband	조직을 해산하다	break up
10	☐ dreadful	무서운	frightful
11	☐ engulf	집어삼키다	overwhelm
12	☐ exemplify	예시하다	demonstrate
13	☐ fawn	아첨하다	grovel
14	☐ fractious	성미가 까다로운	unruly
15	☐ gnarled	울퉁불퉁하고 비틀린	twisted
16	☐ ill-timed	시기가 좋지 않은	inopportune
17	☐ impair	손상시키다	harm
18	☐ intrinsic	고유한	basic
19	☐ invert	거꾸로 뒤집다	overturn
20	☐ lament	슬퍼하다	mourn
21	☐ livid	노발대발한	furious
22	☐ meander[1]	정처 없이 걷다	drift
23	☐ moor	배를 정박시키다	fasten
24	☐ nullify	취소하다	invalidate
25	☐ overpower	이기다	conquer
26	☐ perspicacious	선견지명이 있는	discerning
27	☐ plethora	과다	glut
28	☐ rage	분노	wrath
29	☐ respite	일시적 중지	intermission
30	☐ scald	데게 하다	burn
31	☐ singe	그을리다	scorch
32	☐ stain	더럽히다	soil
33	☐ subtle	미묘한	faint
34	☐ terse	간결한	succinct
35	☐ ultimatum	최후 통첩	final offer
36	☐ vicious	나쁜	spiteful

1	☐ accomplice	공범	associate
2	☐ ambivalent	좋으면서 싫은	conflicting
3	☐ ameliorate	개선하다	improve
4	☐ chastise	벌하다	punish
5	☐ conceited	자부심이 강한	pompous
6	☐ conflagration	대화재	large fire
7	☐ deplete	고갈시키다	exhaust
8	☐ disclaim	부인하다	deny
9	☐ dreary	단조로운	depressing
10	☐ enhance	개선시키다	reinforce
11	☐ exert	힘을 쓰다	apply
12	☐ feasible	실행할 수 있는	possible
13	☐ fervent	열정적인	enthusiastic
14	☐ glutton	대식가	gourmand
15	☐ headstrong	완고한	willful
16	☐ illumination	조명	light
17	☐ incoherent	조리가 안 맞는	rambling
18	☐ innuendo	풍자	insinuation
19	☐ invigorate	기운 나게 하다	stimulate
20	☐ lampoon	풍자문으로 비방하다	satirize
21	☐ lucid	명쾌한	evident
22	☐ meander[2]	굽이쳐 흐르다	wind
23	☐ moot	논란의 여지가 있는	debatable
24	☐ numerous	수많은	myriad
25	☐ overt	명백한	clear
26	☐ pertinent	적절한	suitable
27	☐ pretext	구실	quibble
28	☐ rally	다시 불러 모으다	muster
29	☐ restive	침착성이 없는	fidgety
30	☐ scathing	냉혹한	biting
31	☐ skittish	겁이 많은	edgy
32	☐ stammer	말을 더듬다	stutter
33	☐ succinct	간결한	pithy
34	☐ testy	짜증 잘 내는	touchy
35	☐ upbraid	질책하다	scold
36	☐ winsome	마음을 끄는	appealing

#		한국어	영어
1	☐ accomplished	뛰어난	skilled
2	☐ amble	느긋하게 걷다	stroll
3	☐ atone	속죄하다	repent
4	☐ blueprint	청사진	design
5	☐ comprise	~로 구성되다	contain
6	☐ concerned	걱정스러운	troubled
7	☐ counteract	거스르다	counter
8	☐ deplore	비탄하다	lament
9	☐ disburse	지급하다	expend
10	☐ drench	물에 흠뻑 적시다	soak
11	☐ enigma	수수께끼	mystery
12	☐ exhaustive	철저한	thorough
13	☐ feeble	약한	frail
14	☐ filibuster	의사 진행 방해	obstruction
15	☐ gobble	게걸스럽게 먹다	devour
16	☐ hymn	찬송가	chant
17	☐ impasse	교착 상태	deadlock
18	☐ incompatible	서로 맞지 않는	unsuited
19	☐ inordinate	과도한	excessive
20	☐ invincible	무적의	indestructible
21	☐ leeway	재량	latitude
22	☐ malinger	꾀병을 부리다	dodge
23	☐ morale	사기	spirit
24	☐ obese	비만한	corpulent
25	☐ overture	서곡	prelude
26	☐ peruse	꼼꼼하게 읽다	read
27	☐ prodigal	낭비하는	extravagant
28	☐ ramble	어슬렁거리다	wander
29	☐ resume	다시 시작하다	restart
30	☐ shiftless	아무 의욕이 없는	slothful
31	☐ simultaneous	동시에 일어난	synchronous
32	☐ stance	발의 위치	posture
33	☐ suffice	만족시키다	satisfy
34	☐ theology	신학	religious theory
35	☐ unanswerable	반박할 수 없는	conclusive
36	☐ vigilant	조심하는	wary

1	☐ accord	일치	agreement
2	☐ amenable	말을 잘 듣는	willing
3	☐ atrocity	잔혹 행위	cruelness
4	☐ bluff	허세 부려 속이다	trick
5	☐ chide	꾸짖다	criticize
6	☐ concord	일치	harmony
7	☐ courteous	예의 바른	polite
8	☐ demoralize	사기를 꺾다	discourage
9	☐ discard	버리다	desert
10	☐ divert	기분 전환하다	amuse
11	☐ elevate	올리다	lift up
12	☐ exhibit	보여주다	manifest
13	☐ feign	가장하다	pretend
14	☐ fraternal	형제의	brotherly
15	☐ gossamer	섬세한 거미줄 같은	delicate
16	☐ heave	힘주어 들어올리다	hoist
17	☐ illusory	환상에 불과한	deceptive
18	☐ incongruous	어울리지 않는	inharmonious
19	☐ inquire	질문을 하다	ask
20	☐ invoke	빌다	appeal
21	☐ languid	나른한	listless
22	☐ locomotive	기관차	train
23	☐ morbid	병적인	ghastly
24	☐ obituary	부고 기사	death notice
25	☐ parameter	한도	boundary
26	☐ pervade	널리 퍼지다	permeate
27	☐ pristine	완전히 새것 같은	intact
28	☐ rampant	마구 퍼지는	uncontrolled
29	☐ resurrect	부활시키다	revive
30	☐ scoff	비웃다	mock
31	☐ sink	가라앉다	founder
32	☐ stare	응시하다	gaze
33	☐ suffocate	질식하다	smother
34	☐ therapeutic	치료의	curative
35	☐ unaffected	진실된	sincere
36	☐ vigor	정력	energy

1	☐ acme	절정	summit
2	☐ anomaly	변칙	irregularity
3	☐ attire	의류	apparel
4	☐ bluster	엄포를 놓다	intimidate
5	☐ choleric	화를 잘 내는	irascible
6	☐ concoct	섞어서 만들다	devise
7	☐ covet	탐내다	envy
8	☐ depot	창고	warehouse
9	☐ discerning	통찰력이 있는	discriminating
10	☐ droop	숙이다	stoop
11	☐ enlighten	계몽하다	edify
12	☐ exhilarate	기분을 들뜨게 하다	elate
13	☐ felony	중죄	offense
14	☐ frail	깨지기 쉬운	fragile
15	☐ gourmet	식도락가	epicure
16	☐ hectic	열광적인	frantic
17	☐ illustrate	설명하다	exemplify
18	☐ inconsolable	너무 슬퍼하는	brokenhearted
19	☐ inquisitive	알고 싶어하는	curious
20	☐ involuntary	자기도 모르게 하는	automatic
21	☐ languish	기운이 없어지다	droop
22	☐ lofty	높으신	haughty
23	☐ meddlesome	간섭하기 좋아하는	nosy
24	☐ moribund	다 죽어가는	dying
25	☐ objective	목적	purpose
26	☐ palpable	감지할 수 있는	perceptible
27	☐ petition	청원	request
28	☐ proficient	솜씨 있는	adept
29	☐ ranch	농장	farm
30	☐ resuscitate	(죽어가는 사람을) 살리다	resurrect
31	☐ scornful	조롱하는	derisive
32	☐ skeptical	의심 많은	doubtful
33	☐ stark	적나라한	bleak
34	☐ suite	세트	set
35	☐ threshold	문지방	sill
36	☐ vilify	비난하다	defame

1	☐ accrue	생기다	accumulate
2	☐ amiable	호감을 주는	agreeable
3	☐ attribute	성격	disposition
4	☐ blunt	둔한	callous
5	☐ complexion	안색	appearance
6	☐ congenial	마음이 맞는	compatible
7	☐ crafty	교활한	sly
8	☐ depravity	타락	corruption
9	☐ discreet	신중한	prudent
10	☐ dub	별명이나 호칭을 붙이다	name
11	☐ enmity	적개심	ill will
12	☐ exhort	열심히 타이르다	urge
13	☐ ferment	발효되다	ripen
14	☐ frantic	광란의	frenzied
15	☐ groundless	근거없는	unfounded
16	☐ heed	주의하다	care
17	☐ illustrious	유명한	well-known
18	☐ incorporate	통합시키다	absorb
19	☐ insanity	광기	madness
20	☐ iota	극소량	jot
21	☐ labyrinth	미로	maze
22	☐ log	항해 일지	diary
23	☐ mediate	조정하다	negotiate
24	☐ morose	언짢은	miserable
25	☐ parole	가석방	conditional release
26	☐ petrify	(공포로 돌처럼) 굳게 하다	horrify
27	☐ profound	깊은	deep
28	☐ rancor	깊은 원한	resentment
29	☐ reconciliation	화해	conciliation
30	☐ scoundrel	건달	rogue
31	☐ skinflint	구두쇠	miser
32	☐ stupefy	깜짝 놀라게 하다	stun
33	☐ sullen	뿌루퉁한	surly
34	☐ thrifty	절약하는	frugal
35	☐ uncommitted	어느 편도 아닌	neutral
36	☐ vindicate	정당함을 입증하다	justify

1	☐ accumulate	모으다	amass
2	☐ amicable	우호적인	friendly
3	☐ audacious	대담한	daring
4	☐ blithe	쾌활한	carefree
5	☐ catalyst	촉매	motivation
6	☐ concur	동의하다	agree
7	☐ covert	비밀의	concealed
8	☐ deprecate	비난하다	denounce
9	☐ dubious	의심스러운	suspicious
10	☐ ennui	권태	boredom
11	☐ exile	추방하다	deport
12	☐ ferret	샅샅이 찾아내다	search
13	☐ fraud	속임수	deceit
14	☐ gracious	상냥한	benevolent
15	☐ hegemony	헤게모니	domination
16	☐ imbibe	(술을) 마시다	drink
17	☐ incorrigible	구제 불능의	incurable
18	☐ insatiable	만족할 줄 모르는	voracious
19	☐ irascible	화를 잘 내는	irritable
20	☐ lapse	실수	error
21	☐ loom	보이기 시작하다	appear
22	☐ mediocre	보통의	ordinary
23	☐ motif	(작품 속) 작가의 중심 사상	main idea
24	☐ oblique	비스듬한	sloping
25	☐ pacify	진정시키다	calm
26	☐ plunder	약탈하다	rob
27	☐ progeny	자손	children
28	☐ relocate	이전하다	move
29	☐ retentive	기억이 좋은	holding
30	☐ sabotage	방해 행위	destruction
31	☐ skirmish	작은 접전	fight
32	☐ stately	위엄 있고 웅장한	grand
33	☐ summit	정상	top
34	☐ thrive	번영하다	flourish
35	☐ undaunted	겁내지 않는	indomitable
36	☐ vindictive	악의 있는 복수심을 가진	revengeful

1	☐ acclimate	적응하다	adapt
2	☐ assimilate	동화시키다	accommodate
3	☐ augment	늘리다	increase
4	☐ blurb	짧고 과장된 광고	advertisement
5	☐ chronic	고질적인	incessant
6	☐ conciliatory	달래는	appeasing
7	☐ depreciate	가치를 떨어뜨리다	devalue
8	☐ discursive	두서없는	digressive
9	☐ dulcet	상쾌한	pleasant
10	☐ established	인정받는	accepted
11	☐ exodus	(많은 사람들의) 대이동	evacuation
12	☐ felicity	행복	bliss
13	☐ folly	어리석음	foolishness
14	☐ grandiose	뽐내는	theatrical
15	☐ heinous	혐오스러운	horrifying
16	☐ incarnate	형태로 구현되다	embody
17	☐ increment	증가	addition
18	☐ inscrutable	이해하기 어려운	mysterious
19	☐ irate	분노한	enraged
20	☐ lash	매질	whip
21	☐ loquacious	수다스러운	wordy
22	☐ meditate	명상하다	contemplate
23	☐ motley	잡다하게 마구 섞인	mixed
24	☐ obliterate	지우다	efface
25	☐ pact	약속	deal
26	☐ placid	고요한	serene
27	☐ proliferate	급격히 증가하다	multiply
28	☐ ransack	샅샅이 뒤지다	forage
29	☐ reticent	과묵한	reserved
30	☐ scroll	두루마리	roll
31	☐ slack	늘어진	loose
32	☐ static	정적인	still
33	☐ summon	소환하다	call
34	☐ tranquility	평온함	calmness
35	☐ underhanded	공정하지 않은	dishonest
36	☐ virtue	미덕	goodness

1	☐ abscond	도주하다	leave secretly
2	☐ amorphous	형태가 없는	shapeless
3	☐ auspicious	길조의	propitious
4	☐ boisterous	매우 시끄러운	uproarious
5	☐ chronicle	연대기	annals
6	☐ condemnation	비난	criticism
7	☐ crave	열렬히 원하다	yearn for
8	☐ deputy	대리인	representative
9	☐ disconcert	당황하게 하다	confound
10	☐ dune	모래 언덕	sand dune
11	☐ enthrall	매혹시키다	enchant
12	☐ exonerate	비난에서 해방시키다	absolve
13	☐ fete	축제	gala
14	☐ frayed	닳은	worn
15	☐ graphic	생생한	vivid
16	☐ immaculate	깨끗한	fastidious
17	☐ incriminate	남에게 죄를 뒤집어 씌우다	inculpate
18	☐ iridescent	보는 각도에 따라 색깔이 변하는	lustrous
19	☐ ironic	반대 내용을 의미하는	cynic
20	☐ lass	소녀	girl
21	☐ lore	민간 전승	information
22	☐ mettle	패기	boldness
23	☐ mien	표정	countenance
24	☐ oblivion	망각	forgetfulness
25	☐ pageant	행렬	spectacle
26	☐ poignant	마음 아픈	affecting
27	☐ prolific	많은 작품을 만드는	productive
28	☐ rectify	바로잡다	amend
29	☐ redress	보상	compensation
30	☐ scribe	필경사	copyist
31	☐ slaughter	학살	killing
32	☐ sneaky	교활한	underhanded
33	☐ sumptuous	사치스러운	costly
34	☐ syntax	구문론	arrangement
35	☐ undermine	(명성 등을) 훼손하다	impair
36	☐ vent	통풍구	outlet

1	☐ abate	약해지다	lessen
2	☐ amplify	증폭시키다	enlarge
3	☐ austere	엄격한	stern
4	☐ bearing	태도	conduct
5	☐ chivalry	기사도	courtesy
6	☐ circumspect	신중한	cautious
7	☐ craven	겁 많은	weak
8	☐ deranged	미친	insane
9	☐ discontented	불만스러운	dissatisfied
10	☐ duplicate	복제하다	reproduce
11	☐ earnest	진지한	ardent
12	☐ exorbitant	말도 안 되는	outrageous
13	☐ felicitous	아주 적절한	appropriate
14	☐ freight	화물 운송	carriage
15	☐ gratitude	감사	thankfulness
16	☐ heterogeneous	여러 다른 종류들로 이뤄진	diversified
17	☐ immense	엄청난	gigantic
18	☐ incumbent	재직 중인	official
19	☐ insight	통찰력	discernment
20	☐ irrelevant	관련 없는	immaterial
21	☐ lubricate	기름칠을 하다	grease
22	☐ meek	온순한	compliant
23	☐ motto	모토	proverb
24	☐ obnoxious	몹시 불쾌한	abhorrent
25	☐ poise	마음의 평정	composure
26	☐ prerogative	특권	privilege
27	☐ promenade	산책	leisurely walk
28	☐ rapport	우호적인 관계	relationship
29	☐ retort	반박하다	rejoin
30	☐ scrupulous	양심적으로 열심히 하는	conscientious
31	☐ slay	학살하다	kill
32	☐ stature	키	height
33	☐ superimpose	위에 얹다	lay on a top
34	☐ tribulation	고난	adversity
35	☐ unravel	(직물이나 밧줄 등을) 풀다	solve
36	☐ virulent	맹독의	baneful

1	☐ acquiesce	동의하다	accede
2	☐ analogy	유사	resemblance
3	☐ authentic	진짜의	genuine
4	☐ bore	뚫다	drill
5	☐ churn	마구 휘젓다	stir
6	☐ condole	애도하다	comfort
7	☐ credulous	너무 쉽게 믿어버리는	gullible
8	☐ discord	불일치	disagreement
9	☐ duplicity	사기	artifice
10	☐ entice	매혹하다	allure
11	☐ exotic	이국적인	foreign
12	☐ feat	위업	achievement
13	☐ frenetic	열광적인	maniacal
14	☐ gratuitous	무료의	free of charge
15	☐ herculean	큰 힘이 드는	prodigious
16	☐ immerse	푹 빠지다	submerge
17	☐ incur	초래하다	get
18	☐ insincere	진심이 아닌	hypocritical
19	☐ irrigate	(토지에) 물을 대다	water
20	☐ latent	잠재적인	dormant
21	☐ lucrative	수익이 되는	profitable
22	☐ melancholy	우울한	sad
23	☐ mourn	슬퍼하다	bewail
24	☐ obscene	외설적인	indecent
25	☐ palatable	맛 좋은	delicious
26	☐ polish	닦다	burnish
27	☐ prominent	저명한	distinguished
28	☐ reparation	보상	remuneration
29	☐ revolt	반란을 일으키다	rebel
30	☐ scrutinize	세밀히 조사하다	ransack
31	☐ sleek	매끈한	smooth
32	☐ statute	법령	act
33	☐ supersede	대신하다	displace
34	☐ timid	겁 많은	timorous
35	☐ unflagging	지치지 않는	untiring
36	☐ visage	얼굴	face

1	☐ acquit	무죄를 선고하다	exculpate
2	☐ anarchy	무정부상태	disorder
3	☐ authority	힘	right
4	☐ bottomless	밑바닥 없는	extremely deep
5	☐ circuitous	간접적인	roundabout
6	☐ condescending	거들먹거리는	patronizing
7	☐ coy	수줍어하는	bashful
8	☐ deride	조롱하다	jeer
9	☐ discourse	강연	dialogue
10	☐ dread	두려움	fear
11	☐ entourage	측근	attendants
12	☐ expansion	확장	enlargement
13	☐ fiasco	큰 실수	debacle
14	☐ frenzy	격분	fury
15	☐ grave	중대한	serious
16	☐ hereditary	유전의	inherited
17	☐ imminent	곧 닥쳐올 것 같은	impending
18	☐ indomitable	불굴의	unconquerable
19	☐ insinuation	암시	innuendo
20	☐ irrevocable	취소할 수 없는	irreversible
21	☐ latitude	허용 범위	leeway
22	☐ ludicrous	웃기는	preposterous
23	☐ mellow	부드럽고 원숙한	soft
24	☐ muffle	소리를 줄이다	mute
25	☐ obscure	분명하지 않은	unclear
26	☐ paltry	하찮은	insignificant
27	☐ plausible	이치에 맞는	probable
28	☐ premise	전제	hypothesis
29	☐ ratify	승인하다	approve
30	☐ retreat	후퇴	withdrawal
31	☐ scurry	허둥지둥 달리다	scamper
32	☐ slender	호리호리한	slim
33	☐ staunch	견고한	steadfast
34	☐ supreme	최고의	highest
35	☐ unflappable	침착한	composed
36	☐ unwarranted	부당한	unjustified

1	☐ accost	(위협적으로) 다가가 말을 걸다	approach
2	☐ anatomy	해부	dissection
3	☐ autonomous	자치의	self-governing
4	☐ boulder	크고 둥근 암석	rock
5	☐ circumscribe	제한하다	limit
6	☐ condone	못 본 척 넘어가다	overlook
7	☐ cower	몸을 웅크리다	cringe
8	☐ derivative	다른 데서 유래된	copied
9	☐ discredit	평판을 나쁘게 하다	disrepute
10	☐ dwindle	줄어들다	decrease
11	☐ entrust	책임이나 임무를 맡기다	hand over
12	☐ expedient	쓸모 있는	convenient
13	☐ fickle	변덕스러운	capricious
14	☐ frigid	매우 추운	frosty
15	☐ gregarious	사교적인	sociable
16	☐ heresy	이교도	pagan
17	☐ hysterical	과잉 흥분하는	neurotic
18	☐ indefatigable	지치지 않는	unflagging
19	☐ insipid	재미없는	bland
20	☐ kin	친족	family
21	☐ laudable	칭찬할 만한	meritorious
22	☐ lukewarm	열의 없는	halfhearted
23	☐ memento	기념물	souvenir
24	☐ mundane	평범한	everyday
25	☐ obsequious	아첨하는	fawning
26	☐ pamper	응석받아주다	indulge
27	☐ physique	체격	shape
28	☐ posthumous	사후의	postmortem
29	☐ predicament	곤경	impasse
30	☐ retrieve	되찾다	recoup
31	☐ scuttle	바삐 가다	scurry
32	☐ secede	분리 독립하다	split from
33	☐ steadfast	고정된	steady
34	☐ surly	무뚝뚝한	gruff
35	☐ token	상징	sign
36	☐ unfledged	어리고 경험이 미숙한	inexperienced

1	☐ acrimonious	신랄한	caustic
2	☐ amnesty	사면	immunity
3	☐ avarice	탐욕	covetousness
4	☐ boulevard	넓은 가로수길	street
5	☐ citadel	요새	fortress
6	☐ confer²	조언하다	advise
7	☐ crevice	갈라진 틈	cleft
8	☐ derive	끌어내다	obtain
9	☐ discrepancy	모순	inconsistency
10	☐ eager	열망하는	anxious
11	☐ enumerate	한 명씩 대다	specify
12	☐ expedite	진척시키다	accelerate
13	☐ fidelity	충실	loyalty
14	☐ frivolous	경박한	flippant
15	☐ grotesque	기괴한	bizarre
16	☐ histrionic	연극하는 것 같은	dramatic
17	☐ incidental	부수적인	minor
18	☐ indelible	지워지지 않는	irrevocable
19	☐ insolvent	파산한	bankrupt
20	☐ isolate	격리시키다	separate
21	☐ launch	시작하다	begin
22	☐ lull¹	일시적인 고요	pause
23	☐ menace	협박	threat
24	☐ municipal	도시의	civic
25	☐ philanthropy	자선 활동	charity
26	☐ prerequisite	전제 조건	necessity
27	☐ propaganda	정치 선전	disinformation
28	☐ provisional	임시의	temporary
29	☐ rational	논리적인	sensible
30	☐ recapitulate	정리해 말하다	recap
31	☐ sooty	그을음이 묻은	dingy
32	☐ stealthy	몰래 하는	secretive
33	☐ surmise	추측하다	guess
34	☐ treason	반역죄	disloyalty
35	☐ unflinching	움츠리지 않는	unwavering
36	☐ vital	매우 중요한	essential

1	☐ acumen	(일에 대한) 감각	shrewdness
2	☐ androgynous	양성의	bisexual
3	☐ averse	싫어하는	unwilling
4	☐ bourgeois	중산층의	middle-class
5	☐ cite	인용하다	quote
6	☐ cringe	겁이 나서 움찔하다	recoil
7	☐ derogatory	경멸하는	disparaging
8	☐ discretion	신중함	prudence
9	☐ ebb	썰물이 되다	recede
10	☐ enunciate	명확히 발음하다	articulate
11	☐ expenditure	지출	spending
12	☐ fierce	사나운	ferocious
13	☐ frugal	절약하는	thrifty
14	☐ gratis	무료로	complimentary
15	☐ hiatus	벌어진 틈	lull
16	☐ immune	면역성이 있는	resistant
17	☐ inexorable	멈출 수 없는	relentless
18	☐ insolent	건방진	impudent
19	☐ itinerant	돌아다니는	peripatetic
20	☐ laurel	월계관	distinction
21	☐ lull²	(마음을) 진정시키다	soothe
22	☐ menagerie	서커스 동물들	zoo
23	☐ mural	벽화	wall painting
24	☐ obsessed	사로잡힌	haunted
25	☐ paragon	모범	exemplar
26	☐ pompous	잘난 척하는	pretentious
27	☐ propriety	적절함	etiquette
28	☐ raucous	요란하고 시끄러운	rowdy
29	☐ revenge	복수	vengeance
30	☐ silhouette	검은 윤곽	outline
31	☐ slither	미끄러지듯 나아가다	slide
32	☐ steed	말	horse
33	☐ surpass	보다 낫다	beat
34	☐ toil	힘들게 일하다	strive
35	☐ ungainly	꼴사나운	clumsy
36	☐ vivid	생생한	graphic

1	☐ aggregate	총합	sum
2	☐ allude	암시하다	insinuate
3	☐ avert	눈을 돌리다	turn away
4	☐ boundless	무한한	infinite
5	☐ clamor	시끄러운 외침	commotion
6	☐ crucial	중요한	critical
7	☐ culinary	요리의	of cooking
8	☐ descend	내려가다	go down
9	☐ disdain	경멸하다	despise
10	☐ eccentric	별난	unusual
11	☐ ephemeral	하루살이 목숨의	transient
12	☐ expert	전문가	authority
13	☐ figment	마음속에만 있는 것	illusion
14	☐ fumble	손으로 더듬어 찾다	grope
15	☐ grim	엄한	gloomy
16	☐ hibernal	겨울의	wintry
17	☐ immutable	변경 할 수 없는	unchangeable
18	☐ indemnify	배상하다	reimburse
19	☐ insomnia	불면증	sleeplessness
20	☐ itinerary	여행 일정표	travel schedule
21	☐ lavish	아낌없이 쓰는	sumptuous
22	☐ lumber	쿵쿵 걷다	walk heavily
23	☐ mendicant	거지	beggar
24	☐ murky	어둑어둑한	dark
25	☐ obsolete	낙후되어서 안 쓰이는	outdated
26	☐ plight	역경	dilemma
27	☐ ponder	숙고하다	consider
28	☐ prose	산문	essay
29	☐ rave	극찬의	flattering
30	☐ revenue	수입	income
31	☐ sear	태우다	char
32	☐ slothful	게으른	sluggardly
33	☐ surplus	잉여	excess
34	☐ topple	흔들거리다	fall over
35	☐ unnerving	불안하게 만드는	disconcerting
36	☐ vociferous	큰 소리로 고함치는	clamorous

1	☐ adjudicate	판결을 내리다	settle
2	☐ antipathy	반감	animosity
3	☐ avid	열광적인	passionate
4	☐ bounty	아낌없이 주어진 것	present
5	☐ clarify	명백하게 설명하다	clear up
6	☐ confine	제한하다	restrict
7	☐ cryptic	난해한	puzzling
8	☐ descendant	자손	offspring
9	☐ disenchanted	흥미를 잃은	disillusioned
10	☐ eclectic	선별된	assorted
11	☐ epic	서사시	heroic poem
12	☐ expertise	전문 기술	skillfulness
13	☐ figurative	비유적인	metaphorical
14	☐ frolic	즐겁게 뛰놀다	gambol
15	☐ grimace	표정이 일그러짐	frown
16	☐ hideous	흉측한	repulsive
17	☐ impart	전하다	inform
18	☐ imperious	고압적인	overbearing
19	☐ indict	죄를 비난하다	accuse
20	☐ jabber	지껄이다	chatter
21	☐ lax	느슨한	slack
22	☐ luminous	빛을 내는	bright
23	☐ mentor	현명하고 성실한 조언자	adviser
24	☐ murmur	속삭이다	mumble
25	☐ obstinate	완고한	dogged
26	☐ pallid	창백한	pale
27	☐ ponderous	크고 육중한	cumbersome
28	☐ prospective	장래의	future
29	☐ ravenous	게걸스럽게 먹는	gluttonous
30	☐ reverberation	반향	echo
31	☐ seclude	격리시키다	isolate
32	☐ sentry	보초	guard
33	☐ slovenly	단정치 못한	sloppy
34	☐ supercilious	거만한	condescending
35	☐ torrid	열렬한	fervent
36	☐ unwitting	자신도 모르는	accidental

1	☐ acute	예리한	shrewd
2	☐ adversity	역경	hardship
3	☐ avocation	취미	hobby
4	☐ belittle	하찮게 만들다	detract
5	☐ cardinal	가장 중요한	principal
6	☐ conducive	~에 좋은	helpful
7	☐ culminate	정점에 닿다	climax
8	☐ deserted	버려진	abandoned
9	☐ disguise	위장시키다	camouflage
10	☐ ecstatic	황홀한	euphoric
11	☐ entrepreneur	사업가	administrator
12	☐ epidemic	급속도로 퍼지는	widespread
13	☐ filch	좀도둑질하다	pilfer
14	☐ furnish	설비를 갖추다	supply
15	☐ grimy	때 묻은	soiled
16	☐ hind	뒤의	posterior
17	☐ impartial	공정한	fair
18	☐ indifferent	무관심한	uncaring
19	☐ intractable	다루기 힘든	unmanageable
20	☐ jaded	지칠 대로 지친	exhausted
21	☐ macabre	섬뜩한	frightening
22	☐ mercenary	용병의	greedy
23	☐ mutable	변덕스러운	changeable
24	☐ obtuse	둔한	unintelligent
25	☐ paramount	주요한	foremost
26	☐ plaintive	애처로운	mournful
27	☐ prostrate	엎드린	flat
28	☐ raze	완전히 파괴하다	annihilate
29	☐ revere	숭배하다	worship
30	☐ seditious	선동적인	rebellious
31	☐ sluggish	둔한	lethargic
32	☐ steer	키를 잡다	guide
33	☐ surreptitious	비밀의	furtive
34	☐ torture	고문	torment
35	☐ unprecedented	전례가 없는	unparalleled
36	☐ voluminous	부피가 큰	vast

1	☐ abolish	폐지하다	annul
2	☐ adamant	단호한	unyielding
3	☐ arbiter	결정권자	mediator
4	☐ brandish	휘두르다	wield
5	☐ cleave	자르다	split
6	☐ confiscate	몰수하다	seize
7	☐ cunning	교활한	crafty
8	☐ desist	그만두다	cease
9	☐ disinterested	관심이 없는	impartial
10	☐ ecumenical	세계적인	universal
11	☐ exculpate	무죄를 입증하다	forgive
12	☐ explicable	설명할 수 있는	understandable
13	☐ fecund	비옥한	fertile
14	☐ furor	격렬한 감정	enthusiasm
15	☐ grin	싱긋 웃다	smile
16	☐ hierarchy	계층제	strata
17	☐ impassive	무감정한	apathetic
18	☐ indigenous	토착의	native
19	☐ instigate	자극하다	foment
20	☐ jar	덜컹덜컹 흔들리다	jolt
21	☐ lean	마른	lanky
22	☐ lunge	갑자기 돌진하다	thrust
23	☐ merchandise	상품	goods
24	☐ muddle	뒤죽박죽을 만들다	clutter
25	☐ obviate	미리 막다	preclude
26	☐ pending	미결정인	undecided
27	☐ probation	보호 관찰	apprenticeship
28	☐ recalcitrant	저항하는	disobedient
29	☐ reverie	공상	daydream
30	☐ secrete	분비하다	generate
31	☐ sly	교활한	cunning
32	☐ stern	가혹한	strict
33	☐ surveillance	감시	observation
34	☐ tantamount	~와 마찬가지의	commensurate
35	☐ unremitting	끊임없이 노력하는	unending
36	☐ vile	극도로 불쾌한	disgusting

1	☐ adept	숙련된	skillful
2	☐ animosity	악의	hostility
3	☐ babble	불명료한 소리를 내다	jabber
4	☐ brash	성급한	cocky
5	☐ circumvent	피하다	sidestep
6	☐ cull	골라내다	select
7	☐ cupidity	탐욕	greed
8	☐ desolate	황폐한	dreary
9	☐ dismantle	철거하다	break apart
10	☐ edible	먹을 수 있는	eatable
11	☐ epitaph	비문	inscription
12	☐ explicit	진술 등이 명백한	specific
13	☐ finesse	술책	gimmick
14	☐ furtive	몰래 하는	stealthy
15	☐ glib	구변 좋은	slick
16	☐ hitherto	지금까지는	until now
17	☐ impeach	탄핵하다	incriminate
18	☐ indignant	분개한	choleric
19	☐ integrate	통합시키다	combine
20	☐ jargon	은어	terminology
21	☐ magnate	거물	mogul
22	☐ merger	합병	amalgamation
23	☐ mutter	궁시렁거리다	murmur
24	☐ ordinance	조례	law
25	☐ parry	받아넘기다	avert
26	☐ portal	현관	gate
27	☐ prosaic	평범한	unimaginative
28	☐ rejuvenate	다시 젊어 보이게 하다	revitalize
29	☐ revert	원상태로 돌아가다	degenerate
30	☐ secular	속세의	earthy
31	☐ smack	찰싹 치다	strike
32	☐ stifle	숨을 막다	suffocate
33	☐ susceptible	민감한	responsive
34	☐ towering	우뚝 솟은	colossal
35	☐ unruly	말 안 듣는	recalcitrant
36	☐ vulnerable	약한	susceptible

1	☐ adhere	둘러붙다	stick
2	☐ annex	덧붙이다	add
3	☐ badger	귀찮게 하다	pester
4	☐ bravado	허세	bluster
5	☐ clench	이를 악물다	clinch
6	☐ confront	직면하다	challenge
7	☐ cursory	서두르는	hasty
8	☐ despicable	경멸할 만한	contemptible
9	☐ disposable	일회용의	dispensable
10	☐ edict	명령	order
11	☐ epoch	시대	era
12	☐ exploit	착취하다	abuse
13	☐ flowery	꾸밈이 심한	ornate
14	☐ futile	쓸모없는	useless
15	☐ grisly	소름 끼치게 하는	gruesome
16	☐ hilarious	매우 재미있는	jolly
17	☐ impeccable	결점 없는	faultless
18	☐ indiscreet	무분별한	imprudent
19	☐ instinct	본능	intuition
20	☐ jaunt	짧고 즐거운 여행	excursion
21	☐ kleptomaniac	도벽이 있는 사람	thief
22	☐ lure	유혹하다	entice
23	☐ mercurial	변덕스러운	volatile
24	☐ mutual	상호간의	reciprocal
25	☐ occupy	자리나 시간을 차지하다	inhabit
26	☐ partial	일부의	unfair
27	☐ protrude	앞으로 튀어나오다	bulge
28	☐ rebuff	거절	refusal
29	☐ revile	매도하다	vilify
30	☐ sedative	진정제	tranquilizer
31	☐ smolder	연기만 피운 채 타다	simmer
32	☐ stigma	치욕	dishonor
33	☐ sustain	지탱하다	maintain
34	☐ toxic	유독성의	poisonous
35	☐ unscathed	다치지 않은	undamaged
36	☐ yearn	갈망하다	long

1	☐ adjacent	이웃의	adjoining
2	☐ annihilate	전멸시키다	pulverize
3	☐ baleful	악의적인	malevolent
4	☐ brawl	말다툼	quarrel
5	☐ cliché	진부한 표현	platitude
6	☐ conjecture	추측	surmise
7	☐ curtail	줄이다	reduce
8	☐ debunk	틀렸음을 밝히다	disprove
9	☐ disparage	얕보다	belittle
10	☐ edifice	대 건축물	structure
11	☐ equanimity	평정	aplomb
12	☐ expunge	지우다	erase
13	☐ foible	기벽	defect
14	☐ gale	돌풍	gust
15	☐ groan	신음하다	moan
16	☐ hinder	방해하다	block
17	☐ impede	방해하다	obstruct
18	☐ indiscriminate	무차별의	haphazard
19	☐ insufficient	불충분한	inadequate
20	☐ jaunty	쾌활한	buoyant
21	☐ laudatory	칭찬하는	acclamatory
22	☐ lurk	잠복하다	skulk
23	☐ meritorious	공적이 있는	praiseworthy
24	☐ myriad	무수한	innumerable
25	☐ opus	작품	music piece
26	☐ partisan	열렬한 지지자	devotee
27	☐ prudence	신중	discretion
28	☐ rebuke	비난하다	reprimand
29	☐ reminiscence	추억	memory
30	☐ sedentary	앉아 있는	fixed
31	☐ smug	잘난 척하는	complacent
32	☐ stray	제 위치를 벗어나다	get lost
33	☐ swoop	급강하하다	plummet
34	☐ tether	묶다	moor
35	☐ unseemly	예의 없는	improper
36	☐ waft	풍기게 하다	carry

1	☐ adjourn	연기하다	defer
2	☐ annotation	주석	footnote
3	☐ balk	갑자기 서다	hesitate
4	☐ brazen	뻔뻔스러운	shameless
5	☐ climactic	클라이맥스의	decisive
6	☐ connoisseur	전문가	expert
7	☐ curb	억제하다	restrain
8	☐ despondent	기가 죽은	dejected
9	☐ disparate	본질적으로 다른	dissimilar
10	☐ edify	교화하다	enlighten
11	☐ expound	명확하게 설명하다	explain
12	☐ fissure	갈라진 틈	crack
13	☐ gallantry	용감함	bravery
14	☐ groove	홈	furrow
15	☐ hoard	저장하다	stockpile
16	☐ impending	임박한	imminent
17	☐ indisputable	논란의 여지가 없는	unquestionable
18	☐ insular	배타적인	narrow-minded
19	☐ jettison	버리다	dump
20	☐ legacy	유산	inheritance
21	☐ lush	싱싱한	verdant
22	☐ mesmerize	매혹시키다	hypnotize
23	☐ mystical	신비로운	cryptic
24	☐ odor	냄새	smell
25	☐ pastoral	전원 생활의	idyllic
26	☐ posterity	자손	brood
27	☐ provincial	지방의	regional
28	☐ rebuttal	반박	refutation
29	☐ revoke	취소하다	cancel
30	☐ seep	새어 나오다	ooze
31	☐ snag	예상 밖의 문제	drawback
32	☐ stink	악취를 풍기다	reek
33	☐ swindle	속이다	cheat
34	☐ transcend	초월하다	exceed
35	☐ unswerving	변함없는	undeviating
36	☐ wail	울부짖다	weep

1	☐ adjunct	부가물	accessory
2	☐ anonymous	익명의	unknown
3	☐ banal	진부한	hackneyed
4	☐ bowdlerize	(부적절한 부분을) 삭제하다	censor
5	☐ clinch	확정짓다	decide
6	☐ conscience	양심	compunction
7	☐ daring	대담한	undaunted
8	☐ dictator	독재자	despot
9	☐ disparity	불균형	difference
10	☐ ensign	깃발	flag
11	☐ equilibrium	평형상태	stability
12	☐ exponential	기하급수적인	aggressive
13	☐ fruitful	생산적인	successful
14	☐ gallop	전속력으로 질주하다	bolt
15	☐ hoax	속임수	fraud
16	☐ imperative	피할 수 없는	compulsory
17	☐ indoctrinate	주입하다	brainwash
18	☐ insulate	고립시키다	segregate
19	☐ jeer	조롱하다	boo
20	☐ liaison	연락 담당자	contact
21	☐ luster	광택	glitter
22	☐ memoir	회고록	biography
23	☐ notify	알리다	announce
24	☐ odyssey	장기간의 방랑	trek
25	☐ opulence	풍요	wealth
26	☐ postulate	가정하다	assume
27	☐ quarantine	격리	isolation
28	☐ recede	뒤로 멀어지다	retreat
29	☐ revolve	돌다	rotate
30	☐ seethe	끓어 오르다	boil
31	☐ snicker	킥킥거리다	giggle
32	☐ stingy	인색한	miserly
33	☐ suave	정중한	courteous
34	☐ swivel	회전하다	spin
35	☐ unveil	베일을 벗기다	expose
36	☐ waive	(권리나 주장을) 포기하다	relinquish

1	☐ adroit	노련한	ingenious
2	☐ annul	취소하다	nullify
3	☐ banish	추방하다	exile
4	☐ banter	농담을 주고받다	tease
5	☐ cling	달라붙다	adhere
6	☐ consent	동의하다	assent
7	☐ debonair	세련되고 멋진	elegant
8	☐ destitute	결핍한	needy
9	☐ dispassionate	냉정한	unbiased
10	☐ editorial	사설	opinion
11	☐ equitable	공정한	reasonable
12	☐ exquisite	매우 아름다운	finely detailed
13	☐ flagrant	명백한	blatant
14	☐ galvanize	활기를 띠게 하다	invigorate
15	☐ gross	총합	total
16	☐ hoist	들어올리다	lift
17	☐ imperil	위험에 처하게 하다	endanger
18	☐ indolent	게으른	idle
19	☐ insurgent	반란을 일으킨 사람	mutineer
20	☐ jeopardy	위험	peril
21	☐ legible	알아볼 수 있게 쓰여진	readable
22	☐ methodical	체계적인	systematic
23	☐ modify	수정하다	alter
24	☐ naive	순진한	credulous
25	☐ officiate	직무를 행하다	serve
26	☐ posture	자세	stance
27	☐ provoke	자극하다	incite
28	☐ receptive	수용하는	open
29	☐ rhetoric	수사학	oratory
30	☐ segregate	격리시키다	divide
31	☐ sober	술 취하지 않은	sane
32	☐ stint	아까워하다	scrimp
33	☐ sycophant	추종자	adulator
34	☐ transient	잠시 동안만 지속되는	fleeting
35	☐ unwieldy	다루기 힘든	awkward
36	☐ vanity	자만심	conceit

1	☐ affirmative	긍정의	positive
2	☐ antagonist	적대자	rival
3	☐ barge	무례하게 끼어들다	intrude
4	☐ blasphemy	신성 모독	irreverence
5	☐ clique	한무리	inner circle
6	☐ consecutive	연속되는	successive
7	☐ daydream	백일몽	fantasy
8	☐ detached	사심 없는	disinterested
9	☐ dispatch	급파하다	send off
10	☐ efface	지우다	expunge
11	☐ equity	공평	fairness
12	☐ fair	아름다운	comely
13	☐ flamboyant	현란한	bombastic
14	☐ gentility	고상함	propriety
15	☐ grove	작은 숲	forest
16	☐ hollow	속이 빈	vacant
17	☐ impermeable	액체가 스며들지 않는	impenetrable
18	☐ indubitable	의심할 여지 없는	undoubted
19	☐ intact	손대지 않은	untouched
20	☐ jest	농담하다	joke
21	☐ legion	특정 유형의 많은 사람들	throng
22	☐ magnanimous	마음이 넓은	generous
23	☐ meticulous	꼼꼼한	careful
24	☐ narcissistic	자기 도취증에 빠진	egotistic
25	☐ olfactory	후각의	odorous
26	☐ pathetic	불쌍한	pitiful
27	☐ potable	마실 수 있는	drinkable
28	☐ prowess	용기	skill
29	☐ recondite	많이 알려지지 않은	profound
30	☐ relish	즐기다	enjoy
31	☐ sinister	불길한	ominous
32	☐ sociable	사교적인	gregarious
33	☐ stipend	수당	salary
34	☐ translucent	반투명의	see-through
35	☐ unwilling	꺼려하는	reluctant
36	☐ wane	작아지다	decline

1	☐ admonish	조용히 타이르다	warn
2	☐ anticlimax	실망스러운 결말	letdown
3	☐ barbaric	야만적인	savage
4	☐ broach	언급하다	introduce
5	☐ clumsy	꼴사나운	crude
6	☐ comely	예쁜	attractive
7	☐ consensus	일치	concord
8	☐ detain	못가게 붙들다	confine
9	☐ dispel	쫓아 버리다	disperse
10	☐ efficacy	효능	effectiveness
11	☐ equivalent	동등한	equal
12	☐ exterminate	근절하다	eliminate
13	☐ flammable	불이 잘 붙는	inflammable
14	☐ gape	입을 탁 벌리다	glare
15	☐ grovel	기다	abase
16	☐ holistic	전체론의	complete
17	☐ impetus	움직이게 하는 힘	momentum
18	☐ inducement	유인	incentive
19	☐ intangible	손으로 만질 수 없는	impalpable
20	☐ jocose	익살스러운	jesting
21	☐ legislation	법률제정	enactment
22	☐ magnificent	수려한	superb
23	☐ metropolitan	주요 도시의	municipal
24	☐ nascent	초기의	budding
25	☐ ominous	나쁜 징조의	threatening
26	☐ pariah	추방자	outcast
27	☐ potent	강력한	powerful
28	☐ proximity	(공간이나 시간적으로) 가까움	nearness
29	☐ reciprocal	상호간의	exchanged
30	☐ self-conscious	다른 사람의 시선을 의식하는	nervous
31	☐ soiled	더러워진	smeared
32	☐ stipulation	(필요 조건을 구체적으로) 명시	condition
33	☐ synthesize	합성하다	incorporate
34	☐ travail	고생	toil
35	☐ unyielding	완고한	obdurate
36	☐ warp	휘다	distort

1	☐ adorn	꾸미다	ornament
2	☐ apex	꼭대기	pinnacle
3	☐ aplomb	침착함	poise
4	☐ brood	종족	breed
5	☐ conscript	징집하다	draft
6	☐ consort	배우자	spouse
7	☐ dearth	부족	lack
8	☐ deter	방해하다	impede
9	☐ disperse	흩어지게 하다	scatter
10	☐ egocentric	자기 중심의	self-centered
11	☐ equivocal	모호한	ambiguous
12	☐ extol	극찬하다	praise
13	☐ flicker	깜박거리다	blink
14	☐ gait	걸음걸이	bearing
15	☐ grudging	꺼려하는	afraid
16	☐ homogeneous	동종의	identical
17	☐ implant	꽂아 넣다	insert
18	☐ induction	도입	initiation
19	☐ integrity	진실성	uprightness
20	☐ jolly	즐거운	merry
21	☐ legitimate	합법적인	lawful
22	☐ magnitude	크기	scale
23	☐ midst	중앙	middle
24	☐ natal	출생의	inherent
25	☐ omit	빠뜨리다	leave out
26	☐ patron	후원자	sponsor
27	☐ pine	애타게 그리워하다	longform
28	☐ prudent	신중한	sagacious
29	☐ reckless	앞뒤를 가리지 않는	brash
30	☐ rickety	흔들흔들하는	shaky
31	☐ snobbish	속물적인	stuck-up
32	☐ sojourn	일시적인 체류	visit
33	☐ symmetry	대칭	balance
34	☐ transmute	바꾸다	change
35	☐ upheaval	대변동	disaster
36	☐ wary	조심성 있는	chary

1	☐ antidote	해독제	antitoxin
2	☐ arboreal	나무의	relating of trees
3	☐ bashful	숫기 없는	shy
4	☐ brook	작은 시내	creek
5	☐ clutch	꽉 쥐다	hold
6	☐ conspicuous	눈에 띄는	remarkable
7	☐ deafening	귀가 멀 정도로 큰소리의	earsplitting
8	☐ deteriorate	악화시키다	exacerbate
9	☐ disposition	성질	nature
10	☐ egregious	악명 높은	atrocious
11	☐ era	시대	epoch
12	☐ extort	강제로 빼앗다	blackmail
13	☐ greed	탐욕	avarice
14	☐ grumble	투덜거리다	complain
15	☐ hoodwink	속이다	mislead
16	☐ implausible	사실 같지 않은	impossible
17	☐ indulge	욕망이나 환락에 빠지다	yield
18	☐ integral	없어서는 안 될	vital
19	☐ jolt	갑자기 세게 흔들다	jar
20	☐ leisurely	느긋한	unhurried
21	☐ maintenance	관리	sustenance
22	☐ manifold	많은	numerous
23	☐ munificent	대단히 후한	beneficent
24	☐ omnipresent	어디에나 있는	ubiquitous
25	☐ patronizing	드러내어 선심을 쓰는	snobbish
26	☐ precipitate	촉발시키다	hurry
27	☐ pseudo	가짜의	artificial
28	☐ reckon	세다	think
29	☐ rife	나쁜 것이 만연한	prevalent
30	☐ sensible	지각 있는	level-headed
31	☐ solace	위로	consolation
32	☐ stoic	극기의	impassive
33	☐ sympathy	공감	compassion
34	☐ tier	줄	level
35	☐ uproar	소란	chaos
36	☐ wholesome	건강에 좋은	salutary

1	☐ aboriginal	원주민의	original
2	☐ adversary	적	enemy
3	☐ batch	한 차례 굽는 양	group
4	☐ bent	취향	inclination
5	☐ clutter	어지르다	jumble
6	☐ conspiracy	음모	collusion
7	☐ debilitated	쇠약해진	infirm
8	☐ dejected	낙담한	despondent
9	☐ disprove	잘못되었음을 증명하다	refute
10	☐ egress	출구	exit
11	☐ eradicate	뿌리를 뽑다	root up
12	☐ extenuate	경감하다	diminish
13	☐ extract	뽑다	withdraw
14	☐ garish	지나치게 번쩍거리는	glaring
15	☐ grumpy	퉁명스러운	grouch
16	☐ hospitality	호의	friendliness
17	☐ implement	시행하다	potentiation
18	☐ indulgent	제멋대로 하게 두는	lenient
19	☐ intemperate	절제하지 않는	immoderate
20	☐ jostle	밀치다	shove
21	☐ lengthy	길고 장황한	extended
22	☐ makeshift	임시방편의	improvised
23	☐ milestone	이정표	landmark
24	☐ mint	조폐국	coin plant
25	☐ onset	시작	assault
26	☐ pragmatic	실용적인	practical
27	☐ prolong	연장시키다	extend
28	☐ reclaim	반환을 요구하다	retrieve
29	☐ rigid	엄격한	stiff
30	☐ ruffle	산란하게 만들다	fluster
31	☐ solemn	엄숙한	earnest
32	☐ stolid	둔감한	unemotional
33	☐ synchronize	동시에 일어나다	coordinate
34	☐ trauma	정신적 외상	shock
35	☐ urbane	도시적인	sophisticated
36	☐ waver	흔들리다	sway

1	☐ advent	출현	arrival
2	☐ antithesis	대비	opposite
3	☐ battalion	대대	army
4	☐ buoyant	자신감에 차 있는	perky
5	☐ coalesce	합동하다	unite
6	☐ cohort	집단	company
7	☐ defamation	명예 훼손	libel
8	☐ discriminating	안목 있는	astute
9	☐ disgruntled	불만스러워 하는	discontented
10	☐ elapse	시간이 경과하다	pass by
11	☐ erode	침식시키다	wear away
12	☐ extraneous	관계없는	irrelevant
13	☐ fledgling	풋내기	novice
14	☐ garland	화관	wreath
15	☐ guile	교활	duplicity
16	☐ hostility	적대감	enmity
17	☐ implicate	관련시키다	involve
18	☐ industrious	열심히 일하는	assiduous
19	☐ intriguing	흥미로운	interesting
20	☐ jovial	명랑한	convivial
21	☐ karma	카르마	fate
22	☐ malady	병	illness
23	☐ mill	제분기	grinder
24	☐ nauseous	속이 메스꺼운	queasy
25	☐ onerous	아주 힘든	toilsome
26	☐ porous	구멍이 많은	permeable
27	☐ pry	캐묻다	peep
28	☐ renounce	공식적으로 포기하다	repudiate
29	☐ rigorous	엄격한	severe
30	☐ sentiment	감정	emotion
31	☐ solicitous	걱정하는	mindful
32	☐ stout	뚱뚱한	overweight
33	☐ syndicate	신디케이트	association
34	☐ traverse	가로지르다	Passover
35	☐ usurp	왕위를 찬탈하다	takeover
36	☐ wax	커지다	expand

1	☐ anecdote	일화	episode
2	☐ apathetic	무감각한	nonchalant
3	☐ batter	난타하다	hit
4	☐ bulwark	요새	bastion
5	☐ coarse	거친	rough
6	☐ consummate	완벽의	flawless
7	☐ decant	따르다	pour out
8	☐ detest	싫어하다	loathe
9	☐ disrespectful	무례한	impolite
10	☐ elastic	탄력 있는	resilient
11	☐ erratic	산만한	irregular
12	☐ extravagant	낭비하는	lavish
13	☐ fleet	함대	armada
14	☐ garment	의류	attire
15	☐ gullible	잘 속는	naive
16	☐ hone	연마하다	sharpen
17	☐ implication	함축	suggestion
18	☐ ineffable	말로 표현할 수가 없는	inexpressible
19	☐ intent	몰두하는	determined
20	☐ jubilant	승리에 기뻐하는	triumphant
21	☐ laconic	말을 많이 하지 않는	concise
22	☐ malfunction	오작동	breakdown
23	☐ mendacious	거짓인	untruthful
24	☐ nautical	선박의	maritime
25	☐ onslaught	맹습	attack
26	☐ pecuniary	재정상의	financial
27	☐ primitive	원시 사회의	ancient
28	☐ pugnacious	싸움하기 좋아하는	belligerent
29	☐ relate	~에 대하여 이야기하다	tell
30	☐ sanguine	자신감이 넘치는	optimistic
31	☐ sentinel	보초	sentry
32	☐ straightforward	똑바른	outspoken
33	☐ synopsis	줄거리	abstract
34	☐ treacherous	배반할 것 같은	unfaithful
35	☐ utilize	사용하다	use
36	☐ wilt	시들다	shrivel

1	☐ advocate	옹호하다	champion
2	☐ appease	진정시키다	ease
3	☐ bear	나르다	have
4	☐ bungle	망치다	mess up
5	☐ coin	말을 만들다	create
6	☐ contagious	전염되는	infectious
7	☐ deception	속임	trickery
8	☐ detour	우회로	indirect course
9	☐ disrupt	붕괴시키다	break
10	☐ elated	마냥 행복해하는	jubilant
11	☐ erroneous	잘못된	inaccurate
12	☐ extricate	(위험이나 곤란에서) 구해내다	disentangle
13	☐ fleeting	휘리릭 지나가는	vanishing
14	☐ garnish	장식하다	adorn
15	☐ haggard	초췌한	drawn
16	☐ hovel	오두막	hut
17	☐ implicit	암묵적인	implied
18	☐ injection	주사	dose
19	☐ judicial	사법의	juridical
20	☐ lethal	치명적인	deadly
21	☐ malice	악의	hatred
22	☐ mingle	섞다	mix
23	☐ nebulous	흐린	hazy
24	☐ ooze	새어 나오다	leak
25	☐ pedantic	아는 체 하는	bookish
26	☐ prattle	지껄이다	babble
27	☐ pulverize	가루로 만들다	shatter
28	☐ refined	교양 있는	cultured
29	☐ refute	논박하다	rebut
30	☐ sequel	속편	follow-up
31	☐ solitude	고독	loneliness
32	☐ strain	한계에 이르게 하다	stretch
33	☐ tacit	무언의	silent
34	☐ tread	밟다	step
35	☐ vacillate	결정을 자꾸 바꾸다	waver
36	☐ wispy	몇 가닥으로 된	flimsy

1	☐ aegis	보호	patronage
2	☐ attenuate	약화시키다	debilitate
3	☐ bedlam	대소동	clamor
4	☐ coerce	강요하다	impel
5	☐ constitution	체질	health
6	☐ contempt	경멸	mockery
7	☐ decimate	대량으로 죽이다	exterminate
8	☐ detract	손상시키다	takeaway
9	☐ dissect	해부하다	anatomize
10	☐ elicit	도출하다	bring about
11	☐ erudite	학식 있는	learned
12	☐ exuberant	넘치고 충만한	profuse
13	☐ flick	가볍게 치다	tap
14	☐ garner	얻다	earn
15	☐ grudge	원한	antipathy
16	☐ ignorant	무지한	unaware
17	☐ implore	애원하다	beseech
18	☐ inept	실력 없는	incompetent
19	☐ intercept	가로채다	cut off
20	☐ judicious	분별력 있는	discreet
21	☐ lethargic	늘어진	sluggish
22	☐ malicious	악의 있는	vicious
23	☐ minuscule	매우 작은	minute
24	☐ nomenclature	(학술적) 이름	vocabulary
25	☐ opaque	불투명한	dim
26	☐ pedestal	받침대	podium
27	☐ preamble	서문	preface
28	☐ pun	말장난	wordplay
29	☐ repartee	재치 있는 응답	retort
30	☐ roam	정처 없이 떠돌다	meander
31	☐ sequence	연속	series
32	☐ somber	우울한	dismal
33	☐ taciturn	과묵한	reticent
34	☐ treaty	협정	pact
35	☐ venerable	깊이 존경받는	revered
36	☐ wheedle	감언이설로 꾀이다	coax

1	☐ aesthetic	예술적인	artistic
2	☐ appliance	가전제품	device
3	☐ beguile	속이다	fool
4	☐ burgeon	급증하다	bloom
5	☐ commute	통근	travelworn
6	☐ contemplation	심사숙고	meditation
7	☐ decree	명령	mandate
8	☐ detrimental	해로운	injurious
9	☐ disseminate	흩뿌리다	diffuse
10	☐ effervescent	열광하는	vivacious
11	☐ elongate	연장하다	lengthen
12	☐ exude	흘러 나오다	secrete
13	☐ flinch	주춤하다	wince
14	☐ garrulous	매우 수다스러운	loquacious
15	☐ huddle	되는 대로 모아넣다	crouch
16	☐ immaterial	중요하지 않은	inconsequential
17	☐ inequity	불공정	unfairness
18	☐ interim	당분간의	acting
19	☐ jumble	마구 뒤섞다	disarrange
20	☐ liable	법적 책임이 있는	answerable
21	☐ malleable	두들겨 펼 수 있는	adaptable
22	☐ minute	매우 작은	minuscule
23	☐ negate	부정하다	undo
24	☐ opportune	때가 좋은	timely
25	☐ pedestrian[1]	보행자	walker
26	☐ precarious	불확실한	insecure
27	☐ pungent	강하게 자극하는	piquant
28	☐ repel	쫓아버리다	keep away
29	☐ robust	건강하고 튼튼한	healthy
30	☐ sequester	압류하다	confiscate
31	☐ sonorous	소리가 잘 울려퍼지는	resonant
32	☐ stratagem	책략	plan
33	☐ tackle	달려들다	grip
34	☐ trek	길고 고된 여행을 하다	hike
35	☐ valedictory	고별사	address
36	☐ whet	칼 등을 갈다	hone

1	☐ affable	친근한	amiable
2	☐ apt	~를 잘하는	Inclined
3	☐ behold	보다	look at
4	☐ burnish	윤내다	polish
5	☐ coherent	조리 있는	logical
6	☐ contend	논쟁하다	argue
7	☐ decrepit	노쇠한	weakened
8	☐ devastate	파괴하다	demolish
9	☐ dissent	의견을 달리하다	disagree
10	☐ eloquence	웅변	fluency
11	☐ escalate	단계적으로 확대되다	heighten
12	☐ factitious	꾸며낸	unnatural
13	☐ flippant	경박한	frivolous
14	☐ gasp	헐떡거리다	draw breath
15	☐ hackneyed	진부한	trite
16	☐ hue	색	color
17	☐ imposing	인상적인	impressive
18	☐ inert	스스로 움직일 힘이 없는	inactive
19	☐ interloper	남의 일에 참견하고 나서는 사람	intruder
20	☐ junction	접합점	intersection
21	☐ mammoth	큰	enormous
22	☐ mire	진흙탕	bog
23	☐ negligible	무시해도 좋은	paltry
24	☐ omniscient	모든 것을 다 아는	all-knowing
25	☐ pedestrian²	평범한	mundane
26	☐ precede	앞서다	predate
27	☐ puny	약한	petty
28	☐ repent	후회하다	deplore
29	☐ rod	막대기	pole
30	☐ serendipity	우연히 좋은 일이 일어남	chance
31	☐ specious	허울만 그럴듯한	misleading
32	☐ stratify	층을 형성하다	classify
33	☐ tactful	재치 있는	diplomatic
34	☐ valiant	용감한	intrepid
35	☐ vie	다투다	compete
36	☐ whimsical	변덕스러운	fanciful

1	☐ affectation	그런 척함	feint
2	☐ aggrandize	크게 하다	magnify
3	☐ belie	착각하게 만들다	contradict
4	☐ belligerent	호전적인	hostile
5	☐ cohesion	결합	combination
6	☐ contented	만족한	satisfied
7	☐ decry	비난하다	reprove
8	☐ deviate	빗나가다	diverge
9	☐ dissertation	학술 논문	treaty
10	☐ elucidate	명료하게 하다	clarify
11	☐ eschew	의도적으로 피하다	shun
12	☐ fabricate	거짓말을 꾸며내다	falsify
13	☐ ferocious	맹렬한	barbaric
14	☐ fulfill	수행하다	accomplish
15	☐ heritage	유산	legacy
16	☐ humanities	인문학	liberal arts
17	☐ imposter	사기꾼	charlatan
18	☐ indigent	궁핍한	destitute
19	☐ interlude	사이	interval
20	☐ juncture	중대한 시기	turning point
21	☐ leverage	영향력	influence
22	☐ managerial	관리자의	executive
23	☐ mirthful	즐거운	gay
24	☐ negligent	부주의한	inattentive
25	☐ optimum	최적의	best possible
26	☐ phlegmatic	침착한	undemonstrative
27	☐ purge	축출하다	cleanse
28	☐ puritanical	철저한 금욕주의자의	strait-laced
29	☐ repertoire	연주 가능한 목록	collection
30	☐ serene	고요한	placid
31	☐ sophisticated	세련된	cosmopolitan
32	☐ streak	줄	line
33	☐ tactile	촉각으로 알 수 있는	tangible
34	☐ trenchant	직설적인	incisive
35	☐ validate	정당성을 입증하다	authenticate
36	☐ willful	제 마음대로의	arbitrary

1	☐ affection	애정	fondness
2	☐ ardor	열정	fervor
3	☐ benefactor	후원자	patron
4	☐ cache	은닉처	hideout
5	☐ contentious	논란의 여지가 많은	quarrelsome
6	☐ deduce	추론하다	infer
7	☐ deprive	빼앗다	dispossess
8	☐ deviation	탈선	aberration
9	☐ elusive	교묘히 피하는	slippery
10	☐ esoteric	난해한	abstruse
11	☐ façade	표면	deceptive appearance
12	☐ flounder	버둥거리다	struggle
13	☐ gaunt	매우 마르고 수척한	haggard
14	☐ hail	(손짓이나 소리쳐) 부르다	call to
15	☐ humiliate	굴욕감을 주다	mortify
16	☐ impoverished	가난한	penurious
17	☐ incredulous	쉽게 믿지 않는	skeptical
18	☐ interminable	끝없는	endless
19	☐ jurisdiction	사법권	extent of power
20	☐ liability	법적 책임	answerability
21	☐ magistrate	치안 판사	judge
22	☐ mandate	명령	command
23	☐ nip	살짝 꼬집다	bite
24	☐ nonpartisan	초당파적인	independent
25	☐ pedigree	족보	lineage
26	☐ plague	전염병	pestilence
27	☐ punitive	가혹한	punishing
28	☐ replenish	재충전하다	refill
29	☐ retribution	응징	retaliation
30	☐ semblance	외관	aura
31	☐ souvenir	기념품	memento
32	☐ strenuous	분투의	tiring
33	☐ taint	더럽히다	sully
34	☐ trespass	침입하다	infringe
35	☐ valor	용기	courage
36	☐ wily	꾀가 많은	artful

1	☐ aftermath	여파	consequence
2	☐ apprehensive	걱정되는	concerned
3	☐ blockade	봉쇄	barrier
4	☐ cacophony	불협화음	discord
5	☐ collaborate	함께 일하다	cooperate
6	☐ contort	비틀어서 일그러뜨리다	bend
7	☐ deem	생각하다	regard
8	☐ dilettante	아마추어	dabbler
9	☐ dissipate	없어지다	dispel
10	☐ emanate	나오다	give off
11	☐ esteem	존경	respect
12	☐ facet	다면체	aspect
13	☐ flourish	번성하다	thrive
14	☐ haggle	실랑이를 벌이다	wrangle
15	☐ hunch	예감	gut feeling
16	☐ impregnable	무적의	invulnerable
17	☐ infallible	절대 오류가 없는	unerring
18	☐ intermission	휴식 시간	recess
19	☐ juvenile	소년소녀의	adolescent
20	☐ liberal	관대한	giving
21	☐ maneuver	책략	stratagem
22	☐ miserable	불쌍한	wretched
23	☐ nemesis	이길 수 없는 상대	adversary
24	☐ opulent	부유한	luxurious
25	☐ pernicious	치명적인	detrimental
26	☐ preclude	일어나지 않게 하다	inhibit
27	☐ profuse	많은	copious
28	☐ recoil	움찔하다	flinch
29	☐ roster	근무 표	list
30	☐ savor	맛을 느끼다	relish
31	☐ sovereign	통치자	ruler
32	☐ stride	큰 걸음으로 걷다	march
33	☐ tangible	형체가 있는	real
34	☐ trickery	속임수	chicanery
35	☐ vanquish	정복하다	defeat
36	☐ wince	주춤하다	cower

AMERICAN COLLEGE
VOCABULARY 101

1	☐ agenda	회의 일정	schedule
2	☐ archaic	고대의	antiquated
3	☐ benevolent	자비로운	good
4	☐ cajole	감언이설로 속이다	wheedle
5	☐ congenital	선천적인	innate
6	☐ contradict	부인하다	negate
7	☐ defect	결점	flaw
8	☐ devious	정도를 벗어난	deceitful
9	☐ eavesdrop	엿듣다	overhear
10	☐ eddy	회오리	whirlpool
11	☐ embargo	금수조치	boycott
12	☐ facile	힘들지 않는	simplistic
13	☐ fluctuate	오르락내리락 하다	vacillate
14	☐ genesis	기원	creation
15	☐ hale	건강한	robust
16	☐ harass	괴롭히다	badger
17	☐ impromptu	즉흥적인	extemporized
18	☐ infamy	불명예	notoriety
19	☐ intermittent	간헐적인	sporadic
20	☐ juxtapose	나란히 늘어놓다	place side by side
21	☐ liberate	풀어주다	release
22	☐ maniac	열광자	lunatic
23	☐ miserly	인색한	stingy
24	☐ neophyte	초심자	tyro
25	☐ oracle	신탁	prophecy
26	☐ penchant	강하게 좋아하는 경향	predilection
27	☐ precocious	조숙한	advanced
28	☐ replica	복제본	copy
29	☐ rotund	통통한	stout
30	☐ servile	노예근성의	abject
31	☐ snarl	으르렁거리다	growl
32	☐ subjugate	지배하에 두다	overpower
33	☐ sweltering	무더운	torrid
34	☐ trickle	액체가 뚝뚝 떨어지다	drip
35	☐ vacate	비우다	empty out
36	☐ woe	슬픔	misery

1	☐ aggravate	악화시키다	intensify
2	☐ archipelago	군도	islands
3	☐ bequeath	물려주다	endow
4	☐ colloquial	구어체의	conversational
5	☐ compile	엮다	assemble
6	☐ coterie	소규모 집단	clique
7	☐ defer	뒤로 미루다	put-off
8	☐ devise	고안하다	contrive
9	☐ distaste	불쾌함	disgust
10	☐ emancipate	해방시키다	set free
11	☐ embellish	장식하다	decorate
12	☐ facilitate	일을 쉽게 하다	aid
13	☐ flutter	펄럭거리다	flap
14	☐ genial	친절한	congenial
15	☐ hallow	신성한 것으로 숭배하다	sanctify
16	☐ hurl	세게 내던지다	fling
17	☐ improvise	즉흥적으로 하다	make up
18	☐ infatuated	심취한	obsessed
19	☐ interpose	사이에 끼워넣다	interrupt
20	☐ keen	날카로운	intense
21	☐ manifest	명백한	apparent
22	☐ misery	비참함	distress
23	☐ nestle	편안하게 자리 잡다	snuggle
24	☐ orator	웅변가	speaker
25	☐ penitent	뉘우치는	contrite
26	☐ plod	터벅터벅 걷다	trudge
27	☐ prowl	돌아다니다	roam
28	☐ repose	휴식	restfulness
29	☐ rue	후회하다	regret
30	☐ sever	자르다	cut apart
31	☐ spat	말다툼	dispute
32	☐ spite	앙심	malice
33	☐ tantalize	애타게 하다	taunt
34	☐ trifling	하찮은	trivial
35	☐ vehement	열렬한	zealous
36	☐ versatile	다재다능한	adjustable

MEMO